# The Organ Music of

# Fred Bock

## TABLE OF CONTENTS


Prelude on BE THOU MY VISION (Slane) . . . . . . . . . . . . . . . . . . . . . . 14

Prelude on JESUS, THOU JOY OF LOVING HEARTS (Quebec) . . . . . . . . 22

Prelude on THE LORD'S MY SHEPHERD (Brother James' Air) . . . . . . . . . 19

Prelude on MORNING HAS BROKEN (Bunessan) . . . . . . . . . . . . . . . . . . 4

Postlude on NOW THANK WE ALL OUR GOD (Nun Danket) . . . . . . . . . . 8

Fantasia on ON CHRISTMAS NIGHT (On Christmas Night) . . . . . . . . . . . 27





I0792569

Fred Bock Music Company

# *Thoughts on the music from the composer himself...*

**MORNING HAS BROKEN** *(page 4)*
This piece needs to be rather legato, but not too slow. The 9/4 time signature often makes people think the quarter note is the unit of beat, when it really means that a dotted half is the unit. Use plenty of finger substitution on this one to get the desired legato effect. Rhythmically, lots of give and take. Sing the melody to yourself as you play to keep the tempo at a comfortable and singable speed. I love that last chord...the 4½ octave spread from pedal note C to the top E in the right hand all blend to give a rich, full sound, even at the *ppp* level. Give those harmonics a chance to sound.

**NOW THANK WE ALL OUR GOD** *(page 8)*
The Karg-Elert setting has always been a favorite piece, but I never really felt the chorale melody was very predominant at all. That opening chord and the pedal sixteenth notes which follow rank, in my thinking, as one of the "Ten Great Moments in Organ Literature." My goal was to make more obvious the use of *Nun Danket* so everyone in the pews would recognize the hymntune immediately. Various snippets from Karg-Elert appear throughout this setting, and purists will delight to know that when I "borrowed" from Karg-Elert, I did not change what he wrote. So, if you have dutifully learned the original, playing my setting will not cause any "conflict of interest" to your fingers and feet. Strong and majestic chords at the end should be played *FFF: sforzando* on, trumpets-en-chamade at 16, 8, and 4, please. This piece is dedicated to Diane Bish. Diane, play those last few bars real loud so all those Fort Lauderdale parishioners will clap their hands to their ears, hollering "Enough! Too loud!"

**BE THOU MY VISION** *(page 14)*
Hope your right hand can play the interval of a ninth without rolling the chord. In the opening four bars there's a figure that is repeated several times within the piece. The lift between the repeated notes must be ever-so-smooth. Play these like a violinist would play, on one bow. Do not make it sound harsh or hard, or like two downbeats: instead, play with gentleness of purpose. Select the tempo that suits you best; try using the third score of page 15 as your guide. When those left hand eighth notes sound smooth, the tempo is probably about right. The bottom of page 16 should be rather stately and majestic as the piece moves in those directions and takes on those characteristics. Of course, the next tricky part is sustaining the right and left thumbs holding the E and D while the remaining fingers play other things at the same time. And I hope your organ console is placed so that the congregation can actually *see* you playing the melody with your feet. Folks in the pew like that stuff, and it's a shame to waste it hidden behind a modesty railing or tucked away up in a balcony! And if you play this as a prelude, follow it immediately with a choral Call to Worship sung *a capella* by the choir, starting in the key of D. (For instance, Will James' *Sing and Rejoice,* H.T. FitzSimons Company.) Start the choir *a capella* solidly in the echo of the organ's last chord, which just so happens to be a solid D major chord: this effect can be electrifying for congregation and choir singers alike. Try it.

**THE LORD'S MY SHEPHERD** *(page 19)*
I have dedicated this piece to my wife, Lois, who, even though she doesn't know swell from great about organs, seems to like what I write. Besides, I've never dedicated a piece to her. Lois, this one's for you. (Being arranger and publisher has its privileges!) *Dolce* is the word I use to describe how I'd *like* to hear this piece played. The chord progressions in this one are what charm me most and make *The Lord's My Shepherd* my favorite in this collection. If you like the chordal creativity of folks like George Shearing, Dave Grusin, David Foster, Johnny Mandel, Michael Feinstein, or Paul Winter, then my guess is that you'll probably like this setting of *Brother James' Air.* Be sure you "own" this piece (that means being able to play it with confidence d assurance) before presenting it in public. These are a few of my favorite things: page 20, bar 3; all of page 21, but especially bars 2, 3, 4, 8, 11, and 12. Oh, one other thing: please do not ever ask me to listen to you play this piece unless you have every note down pat just like I wrote it. If you feel constrained to edit and change what I've written, *Don't!*

**JESUS, THOU JOY OF LOVING HEARTS** *(page 22)*
At weddings or funerals when I play this setting, I usually play the J.S. Bach *Prelude and Fugue in e minor* first, and then launch into my piece. The contrasts are most arresting: from contrapuntal to chordal, and the nice key sense that comes from e minor to E major gives everyone a nice lift. Note that this entire piece is to be played on one manual. Use whatever finger substitution you deem necessary to make that repeated chord progression, E-Bb-Db-E-Db-Bb-E, to sound ever-so-smooth, with a slight and gentle crescendo/diminuendo. I enjoy new and unusual treatments of the hymntunes I've known for years, and I hope you appreciate a little ear-stretching now and then as well.

**ON CHRISTMAS NIGHT** *(page 27)*
Not a Christmas can go by without using Richard Purvis' *Greensleeves.* I first heard this as a teenager at a candlelight Christmas Eve service. I'd never heard such rich harmonies in church before! I got hold of a copy of the music right away so I could analyze those gorgeous chord progressions. Well, I hope Mr. Purvis is pleased with the harmonies of *On Christmas Night,* because I dedicate this piece to him. I've been a fan of Richard Purvis for many years, going back to the mid 1960s when I worked for Word Records, and recorded Purvis playing his own compositions at the great Aeolian-Skinner organ at Grace Cathedral in San Francisco. (Trivia afficionados will recall the liner notes to that album dealt with the fresh-squeezed orange juice dilemma at the Fairmont Hotel!) But I digress: it's best if you have long fingers to execute the melody on the Great and still be able to "help out" the left hand playing the accompaniment on the Choir, yet keeping everything sounding smooth and correct. Now those last six bars I leave up to you. If you have a gallery division or speaker, here's the spot to use them. Also up to you is that last "boop" from the pedal played by the right foot. It seemed like a good idea at the time I wrote this setting. How about a soft chime note there instead? Surprise me.

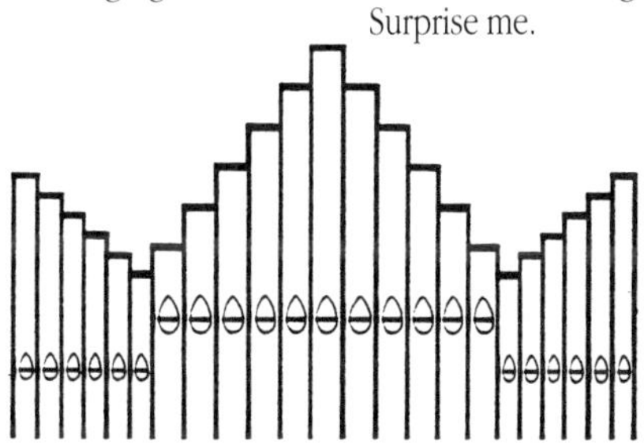

Mr. Bock is currently Director of Music at First Presbyterian Church of Hollywood, California. He also plays arranges, and directs music for recording sessions for albums, commercials, and motion pictures. He was Editor of *Hymns for the Family of God* hymnal (over three million copies in use). His anthems and organ settings are used in churches the world over. The organ publications of his various publishing firms are many and varied and reflect his eclectic tastes in things musical. See page 32 for a listing of publications: from Bach to Langlais to Gordon Young, to Sowerby, and back to Bock again.
This book is the first in a series being planned by the publisher. We suggested to Mr. Bock that he write one organ book a year, and so far, he has agreed. We'll keep you posted.

The Publishers
March, 1991

*for Walt Strony*

Prelude on

# MORNING HAS BROKEN

(Bunessan)

Sw. Light Reed 8′, tremolo optional
Gt. Ch. to Gt., Stopped Diapason 8′
Ch. Strings and Flutes 8′, 4′ to balance Sw. Reed
Ped. Flutes 16′, 8′ to balance, Ch. to Ped.

Traditional Gaelic Melody
*Arranged by Fred Bock*

**Warmly, with feeling**

Ch.
ten. ten. ten.
Gt.
ten. ten. ten.
ten. ten. ten.
a little stronger

r.h.
f
rit.
mp
a tempo
mp
rit.
mf
mp

*for Diane Bish*

Postlude on

# NOW THANK WE ALL OUR GOD

(Nun Danket)

Sw. Full organ, light reeds and mixtures
Gt. Full organ, Gt. to Gt. 4′, Sw. to Gt.
Ped. Strong pedal to balance: 16′, 8′, 4′

Based on material by
Sigfrid Karg-Elert
and Johann Crüger
*Arranged by Fred Bock*

**Stately and majestically**

Sw.
Gt.
f

tr
ff
ff

Sw.
tr
Gt.

tr
brilliante

fff
tr
Add sfz

*for Kimo Smith*

Prelude on

# BE THOU MY VISION

(Slane)

Sw. Salicional, Rohrflute,
additional strings and flutes to taste 8′, and 4′
(Prepare Sw. Reed solo stop)
Gt. Full organ: no reeds or mixtures
Ch. Flutes and/or light Diapasons to balance Reed
Ped. Flutes 16′, 8′, Ch. to Ped.

Traditional Irish Melody
*Arranged by Fred Bock*

mf
Ch.
Sw. (Reed)
mf

mf
Majestically
Gt.
f

(add Sw. Reed to Ped.)
ff
(off Sw. to Ped.)
detached
(add Gt. to Gt. 4′)

ff (add big Reeds)
ten.
ten.
ten.
(add Sw. to Ped.)
(add pedal Reeds)
ff

*for Lois*

Prelude on

# THE LORD'S MY SHEPHERD

(Brother James' Air)

Sw. Flute 4′, Nazard 2 2/3′ (tremolo?)
Ch. Strings 8′ (4′?) to balance, Flute celeste 8′
Ped. Bourdon 16′, light Flute 8′

Traditional English Melody
*Arranged by Fred Bock*

Ch.
(add Ch. to Ch. 4′)
mf

f
mf
mp
mp
ten.
Sw.
tremolo off
(Reduce Ch.) p
ten.
ten.
rit.
pp

*for Chris Elliott*

Prelude on

# JESUS, THOU JOY OF LOVING HEARTS

(Quebec)

Sw. Full, rich Strings, Celestes 8′, 4′
light Flute 8′, (perhaps Sw. to Sw. 4′?)
Ped. Flutes 16′, 8′ to balance

Henry Baker
*Arranged by Fred Bock*

mf
Stronger
f
a little faster
rit.
a tempo

f
mf
ten.
ten.
smoothly
mf

mp
p

*for Richard Purvis*

Fantasia on

# ON CHRISTMAS NIGHT

(On Christmas Night)

Gt. 4′ Flute
Ch. Strings, Celestes, to balance
Ped. Bourdon 16′, light Flute 8′

Traditional English Melody
*Arranged by Fred Bock*

ten.
ten.
ten.
Gt. mf
Gt.
Ch.
Ch.
Ch.
+4′ Coupler

a tempo
f
Gt.

mf
Ch.
mf
Gt.
Ch.

Gt.
Ch.
Ch.
mf
Gt. Soft 4′ Flute, no tremolo
pp
p
pp
(soft chime?)